SCRANTON LACE

SCRANTON LACE

—— poems ——

MARGOT DOUAIHY

ILLUSTRATIONS BY BRI HERMANSON

Dear Jay
Thanks for your generative
energy, for setting things
aflame. Cheers to
adventure.

Margot

CLEMSON
UNIVERSITY
PRESS

Published by Clemson University Press in Clemson, South Carolina.

This book is set in Adobe Minion Pro.

Editorial Assistant: Abigail Maxim

For information about Clemson University Press,
please visit our website at www.clemson.edu/press.

Library of Congress Cataloging-in-Publication Data
Names: Douaihy, Margot, author. | Hermanson, Bri, illustrator.
Title: Scranton Lace: Poems / by Margot Douaihy; illustrations by Bri Hermanson.
Description: Clemson, South Carolina: Clemson University Press, 2018. |
Includes bibliographical references and index.
Identifiers: LCCN 2017021287 | ISBN 9781942954477 (pbk. : alk. paper)
Classification: LCC PS3604.O89435 A6 2017 | DDC 811/.6--dc23
LC record available at https://lccn.loc.gov/2017021287

TABLE OF CONTENTS

❖

DERELICT: Abandoned, as by the owner or guardian; uninhabitable; doomed

SPACE: A blank area in text; dimensions of height, depth, and width within which all things move

CUTTERS

If Trish didn't show me how to angle the broom
I'd never know. All June I shadowed her
at Scranton's Fine Cuts,
the first time a head rested in my hands.
I swept, folded towels, washed scalps,
could not find the right pressure.
Dye and acetone itched my nose.
Heat jammed the windows shut.
No one could open them, not even Danny.
I saw Jesus wink twice on Sister Ann's broach.
Dire Straits on the radio: "Money for nothin'
and chicks for free." I walked home after close,
showered until water ran cold. Scrubbed
my skin raw, but could not get rid of the hair.
It tickled everywhere, under my new bra,
underwear, between my legs, places I heard
lovers slid fingers. I imagined Trish's tongue there.
Needed two jobs to replace the bike
I crashed after smoking my neighbor's hash.
Everyone back from Vietnam had a stash—
you just had to guess where it hid.
A man with a beard stared upside down
as I soaped his red head. *You're awful*
young to be a cutter, he smiled.
I bet you blow-dry, though. Pretty girl
like you. So easy for a razor to slip,
slit a throat. *Too hot,* Sister Ann said
when I washed her. *Too hot.*
Black veil sulked in her lap
like an expired coupon, too old

to be used. Her eyes glued tight
under ceiling light as I massaged
her white roots. *Back to front,*
Trish taught me, *behind the ears.*
Ride the veins. Harder.
Dire Straits on the radio again,
"little faggot with the earring and the make-up."
I sang along even though I could not sing.
Bleach churned the air. Danny and Trish cut
while I swept. Hair fell on our feet, I swept.
All summer I swept as hair spilled,
dumb and stubborn as blood.

AVON

The first married woman
I ever kissed was named Lane
in Scranton's only gay bar
tucked between The Lace

and jail. She was 5'9",
blond, sold Avon.
Whatcha drinking? I asked.
Whatever's clever, she said.

I liked her hoop earrings,
gold ring singing
against the glass
of her happy hour gimlet.

I hung on every word she said,
elbows glued to the warped
bar railing as she decoded
a sad future in my palms.

At 10 we paid the tab,
played make-over
in her car. *Try this.*
Dire-red kiss marks

on the back of my hands
smirked like chaperones,
droning Greek chorus
before a great flood.

She showed me how
to blot and blend, stretch
shadows with the pad
of my middle finger.

If Avon made mascara that didn't run,
she said as she held open my eye,
I'd sell it forever. But it runs, hon,
and at some point, we all cry.

STAGE DIRECTIONS

1
a light stutters on
nour turns the lever
bends the floor toward her
the world beyond
the factory window
leaf-red with autumn
how can so much falling
be so silent she wonders
beginnings hide everywhere
even inside endings

SCRANTON LACE

Broken windows fake awake
like marble eyes, lids locked
after the heart stops. Scranton Lace,
elegant ruin, abandoned since her last
bell rang, cutters fired mid-shift.
Time untied when the big clock broke.
Don't fix it. Why try? There's no next
act when you're used. Despite fine
wreaths, doesn't every graveyard
choke with weeds? Headstones so bored
the undead aren't sure where to haunt;
dates faded, names imbibed by granite.
In Vulgar Latin, Lace means *entice*,
ensnare. The factory tricked me every day
as I drove to school, gutters buckling
with pigeon nests. Grandest banisters
in town flaking rust. Dust, love letter
of age, how dare you. Lace lives
in rewind, tin migraine of a glue high.
Each loom taunted by memories of spin,
gears desperate to grind. What is a blade
but an ache to cut? No money to repair it,
tear it down. Welcome sign still floats
above closed doors like elixir so old
it's turned to poison, slow stripping inside.
In the parking lot, I slept off my first
hangover, learned how much whiskey
I needed to black out: one fist. I fell in lust
with the waitress at the diner behind The Lace.

We kissed in her trailer Friday nights
when her boyfriend hit the late shift.
She called me T. *Because I'm trash?* I asked.
Because you're tiny, she laughed.
Your hands, they're so small.
After she came in my mouth,
she pressed my face to her stomach
which pulsed like a second, weaker heart.
She was new to women—I was barely one—
but we understood lace, negative space,
code of openings, frames blinking
between braids. Lace is a woman
who is here and nowhere, intact but full of holes.
Lace is an old curse and after the reverse spell
the ruined part of you never fits quite right.
Lace is a ruse, see-through, a two-sided
mirror; so many faces hiding within one.

LOOMING

A pantoum

Every mirror shows the world backwards—
smoke, moonlight, rain, lace.
Does a machine sleep, even when it's off?
Turn the knob any further and it will break.

Smoke, moonlight, rain, lace:
Loom means looping. Looming, a specter.
Turn the knob any further and it will break.
Who rewrites text when textiles rename?

Loom means looping. Looming, a specter.
A stitch is the marriage of pierce and pull.
Who rewrites text when textiles rename?
Lace hides inside its own riddle.

A stitch is the marriage of pierce and pull.
Like the escape hatch in the secret past of the factory,
lace hides inside its own riddle.
Only women in our room. Looms tall as Father Ted.

Like the escape hatch in the secret past of the factory.
Sister Ann recites bible stories as we work.
Only women in our room. Looms tall as Father Ted.
Homesickness means monarchs dying mid-flight.

Sister Ann recites bible stories as we work.
I read with my ears; words curl like lace.
Homesickness means monarchs dying mid-flight.
Night is a pattern that is always too tight.

I read with my ears; words curl like lace.
Whenever I breathe I feel two of me.
Night is a pattern that is always too tight.
Please, timepiece, please. Stay still.

Whenever I breathe I feel two of me.
Does a machine sleep, even when it's off?
Please, timepiece, please. Stay still.
Every mirror shows the world backwards.

COMPOSER

i am haunted by what i cannot hear,
glow below the gilded,
last ring of echo.
the trick of lyric:
if it is to breathe, a song
must stay incomplete,
one cutting saved
for replanting,
like a new canvas
hiding inside every
dry brushstroke.
why do i still hold space
in rooms, on walls
for sound, the only art
that cannot be framed?

2
through fine curtains
in the factory's showroom
nour steps
threads against her face
spell holy holy
how terrifying she thinks
to be connected by holes
yes lace is porous
but it can still smother
maybe the space between
is the breath of all textiles
like the lake of white
electrifying the eye

STRAIGHT PINS

When you started you couldn't stop.
Keg-stand queen two years in a row.

No one knew how a small girl could drink so much.
The whole football team wanted under your blouse.

With the hash smoked, Cat claimed your bed. Joe, the sofa.
You pulled me to the rug, used your mom's lace drapes

as blankets, white panes with pins so straight and fine
we didn't see. *What's the difference between blinds*

and drapes? I asked, high enough to hear lace breathe.
Blinds are hard, you said, *drapes are soft. Feel?*

I would've taken off my dress that night, done anything
you wanted. We didn't talk about it. Didn't know how.

We slept past noon. Pins burned, stabbed my arms as I turned.
Like love, like bad drugs, if it doesn't hurt you never learn.

RUNAWAY

The first time I left we were 10. Our house was too small,
too big: hallways spilled into stairwells, gauzy rooms we
never entered, paintings we were too young to decode,
but some we liked better than others. I was the only twin
who needed alone time, spent hours in the bathroom on
the ledge of the tub. I stared into the mirror, black lacquer
frame painted with two gold birds. It claimed the wall like
a crucifix—the best dark place I never hid. Stared until my
eyes burned, until something churned. I emerged from the
mirror, strode into the kitchen declaring: *I'm running away!*
Mom, fantastically ringed, returned to her wontons. Dad
nodded. *Better bundle up then.* You stood in the doorway &
blocked me. *No!* You stamped your feet. *What will you eat?*
Beyond the door, delicate snow erased sidewalks & curbs.
You cried, tried to reach across the doorway like a gate.
Who will you talk to? Now, when I think about us, I see
your small arms, too scared to let me go into the unknown,
& me, too scared not to.

LOGIC

LACE fooled me into thinking an empty center could HOLD

HOLD music on the phone inspires me to give the FINGER

FINGER movements under sheets are pounced on by CATS

CATS prevent me from OVERSLEEPING

OVERSLEEPING helps me waste TIME

TIME is the only remedy for broken HEARTS

HEARTS are reliable as ships made of LACE

LACE fooled me into thinking an empty center could HOLD

3
nour makes space at her table
for elizabeth the new girl
elizabeth the new girl
reminds nour of someone
she's not sure who
yes the moon is a face
but the face of no one you know
like storms changing
the sky the same different
way every time

BLUE MONDAY

There's only one blue that makes you salivate, only one blue that makes you heave. The neon blue of the 1980s. Hue of mall bangs, elixir of anti-freeze. Not "The Blues," just blue. The half-smile trick of faking it. In the late '80s, when even shoulder pads had shoulder pads, I knew I was ugly. My twin was pleasant enough, but I was hideous, or at least forgettable. Why else I would I be so numb? Blue-eyed boys could barely keep their skin on. Girls writhed in Electric Youth. Windows down in the cobalt Jetta we lip-synced "Tell me now how should I feel," lyrics so overplayed they only hinted at an origin, like cyan tides in a video game sea. Cool Ranch Doritos stained my throat. Arctic eye-shadow smeared just so. I didn't know what I wanted back then because it had no name. In the blue tractor beam of night the only white was my acid-washed jeans. In every acid bath is the gift of chemistry: lose part of yourself to become something new. Dye first to start over. Though there's no do-over in the moldy gym at the Winter Ball when I swayed alone to *Blue Monday*, too scared to reach for any hand, even my own.

STAIN

A mirror is my favorite artist:
it breaks if thrown but dances as it breaks.
Wicks that burn clean make me sick.
I need an old fuse with a fussy spark.
Perfection is a prison; lace gets stained
when it lives outside its box.
Lose the flashlight. Give me a pickaxe
so every trick I use to scale the peak
will leave a record. Let the monster follow,
the way my boss trailed me into the bar
to fire me from my Campus Safety job.
From 7pm-3am, in my beige uniform,
I walked scared students across dark lots,
jump-started cars, broke up fistfights.
Bleeding is a good story if you time it right.
The only job I got fired from was my favorite job.
Waiting for dispatch at a bar was against the rules,
so when my beige boss saw me drinking Yuengling,
beeper clipped to my Campus Safety jacket,
he fired me on the spot.
How taut one must be to fire oneself out of a rifle,
how organs would tremble as the trigger kicks.
The only job I got fired from was my favorite job.
My boss's beige eyes laughed as he fired me—
Well, well. Now someone's résumé is stained.
Yes, I'm a fuck up, but isn't rust proof of friction,
rain's dedication? A stain is the lens
that lets us see the moment and in the DNA
we (you, me, the beige boss, the gear and loom,
every clock-hand little or big) all chase ourselves.

The only job I got fired from was my favorite job.
In a universe braided by weft, threaded with X,
why can't I be impaled by the need to unheal?
Kiss me like you want to unlock or eat me
or don't kiss me at all. A latch-hook needle
kidnaps the stitch to set the pattern free.
Safety Officer D, need ya in Tower C for a lockout. Copy.
An override? Copy.
The only job I got fired from was my favorite job.
It's the stain not the atom that holds cells together:
cathedral of red glass, incense so fierce parishioners faint.
Watch lace close enough and you will learn
obsession, the silent repeat that carves space,
like the undulation of gills.
Fire me from Campus Safety, rehire me,
bite me if you want,
just leave a goddamn mark.

GUTTED

October is lit within, a copper pulse,
screaming like a penny taped to the track
of a train that may or may not come.
Twilight's battery acid flu.
Scranton asphalt doesn't point back
or ahead. No math for a half-life.

Let me show you how clean it could be,
        half-dead factory, walls gutted to stud.
Let me put my mouth on the sting, suck out
        the poison—bone licked bald.
Let me feel it, brackish blood in the gums
        after a hit hard enough to hear stars.

Like the window jamb we snuck through to huff glue,
I've rusted too often to open or close smooth.
Weather wraps around, though I want it inside,
to kill or cure. It's fall now, but isn't it always?
The cricket call—a voice with no name—
steals the space between before and after.
Even the moon is dented,
but she still turns her face to the wind.

4
before work the factory girls attend mass
father ted says the senses lie
rely on your mind
then father ted says the mind can't decide
rely on your senses
nour heals her bleeding finger
by sucking the tip dry
sunlight streams in
painting the new girl's hands
elegant fingers untorn despite the loom
nour wonders if light lies
or light tells the truth

THE FIFTH ELEMENT AT THE RITZ DOWNTOWN

In the back row we fell
with Leeloo into the future.
Wild hair and feral eyes.
The blue Diva hypnotized us.
I watched you in the dark, in love
with the way a woman's face
is exquisite when terrified.
It was the summer
before the theater closed.
We hadn't come out yet
to each other or ourselves.
I borrowed my mom's caravan
to drive you to work at the mall.
Dusk turned the sky bitten-lip pink.
The air conditioner wouldn't get cold,
so you held ice cubes
from your Mountain Dew
against my neck.
The Fifth Element showed monks
talking to stones. We rolled a blunt
from a cigar stub you dug out
of a gas station ashtray.
One hit and I choked so hard I cried.
You were always doing that,
daring me to stay in my body.
Now if I notice Diva blue
I look at it hard, the way you
took your sunglasses off and
stared at the sun until your eyes stung.
Light that does not last
blinds you into seeing it forever.

ALTERNATIVE FACTS

If you don't like the way a sound sounds
just rearrange the vowels
or better yet the consonants.
Say *consonants* three times fast
and it becomes *consequence.*
My favorite consequence
is in the movie about the camp
for kid astronauts.
The robot loves its human friend so much
it launches the human into the galaxy.
Drowning in ether is one consequence of love.
Riding a fireball is another.
The movie's synth soundtrack
is as ecstatic as a punch
to the back of the heart
as teens spin in the aerotrim.
I'd like you to flip me like that,
over and over, all horrid beauty,
like an axe blade
looping into the bullseye.
I can't say that it will turn out okay.
I'm not sure what's up or down anymore,
but I still want to be loved hard,
pushed off the edge
into the deep well of the possible.

THE BOOK OF LACE

1. BIRTH OF THE NEEDLE

Inside the sky was the storm and inside the storm
was the lightning bolt and inside the lightning bolt
was the seam and through the seam was the bird
and on the bird was the wing and under the wing
was the hand and on the hand was the palm
and written on the palm was the scar
and inside the scar was the scream
and inside the scream was the flame
and inside the fire was the stone
and inside the stone was the storm
and watching the storm was the woman
and inside the woman was the bone
and inside the bone was the hole
and inside the hole was the need.

2. BIRTH OF THE CUT

A needle is the enemy of skin
/ skin is the ally of the circle
A circle is the enemy of the zag
/ zag is the ally of the zig
A zig is the enemy of water
/ water is the ally of loam
Loam is the enemy of air
/ air is the ally of fire
Fire is the enemy of fashion
/ fashion is dictated by the Queen
The Queen demands a coronet
/ a coronet of living light
The maidservant peels her skin

3. Birth of the Pattern

Stop feeding the clock
so its hands starve and
devour the notches near them.
Fears of being forgotten
by time will trick your heart.
False-starts stop breath.
Breath is sticky,
fools your brain
into fainting.
To fall is to start over.
Starting over is the only poem,
the only pattern
you've memorized.

4. Birth of Dyeing

Maidservant 2
I like can't believe that the Queen like licked the poisoned paper.
Maidservant 1
How sticky the poison ink dripping
from the corners of mouth! Like tapped sap!
Maidservant 3
She didn't *lick* the poisoned letter. She *kissed* it.
Maidservant 2
Like why would the Queen like kiss paper?
Maidservant 3
She thought the letter was from the King.
Maidservant 2
Aww. That's like so sweet.

Maidservant 1

Well, all the same, she is hardcore DYING in the tower!

Maidservant 3

Why are we here? We were nowhere near the Queen
when she took in the False Mail.

Maidservant 1

Always close to Queen we are! In our hearts with Queen are we!

Maidservant 2

What like does that like even mean?

Maidservant 1

We will stay chained in the tower until the killer is caught!

Maidservant 2

What will they like do to him when they like find
the Queen's killer?

Maidservant 3

Behead him.

Maidservant 1

Cut him open to show how evil has charred his heart!
Singed like a pig on a spit!

Maidservant 2

They cannot like cut open a man.

Maidservant 3

Sure they can. They invented knives last year.

Maidservant 2

Like what do you mean "they" like "invented" "knives" last year?

Maidservant 3

They made something new. Something that does something
that could not be done without that thing they just made.

Maidservant 1

As the glass eye of the microscope sees the baby apple
growing inside of the seed inside of the spine of the mother apple!

Maidservant 3

It's a *core*, not a spine, but yeah, kinda something like that.

Maidservant 1

Never do YOU ask for the thoughts of ME but I have worthy
thoughts TOO!

Maidservant 3

I'm sure.

Maidservant 2

She like totally does. I like have thoughts, too. We like all do.

Maidservant 1

Ha! Queen One is SO un-alive!

Maidservant 2

We're like totally going to like die in here.

Maidservant 3

Yep.

Maidservant 1

Uh-oh!

Maidservant 2

Maybe we can like change our colours and like escape the tower
in a rug or dung wagon.

Maidservant 1

Let's change our colours! One, two, three! Nothing changed!

Maidservant 3

If I could be reborn I'd be the key that unlocks us
from this fucking tower.

Maidservant 1

If I could be reborn I'd be a glass eye that can sees inside insides!

Maidservant 2

I'd like be a hawk and like fly outta here. No, I'd like be the sky.

Maidservant 1

I'd be lightning!

Maidservant 2
I'd like be a lightning bug.
Maidservant 1
Lightning bugs make people smile!
Maidservant 3
You'd only live for one day if you were a lighting bug.
Maidservant 1
At least you could feel smiled upon even if for a moment quick!
You change moods just by flying near!
Maidservant 2
Like you were a sun.
Maidservant 1
A sun!
Maidservant 3
Yes, a sun.

5. Birth of the Knot

YES. QUEENS FROM RIVAL KINGDOMS
ARE HAVING AN AFFAIR
WHILE THEIR KINGS JOUST
FOR CONTROL OF ALL FIEFDOMS.
CRAZY, RIGHT? BUT OPPOSITES ATTRACT.
DIFFERENT CLANS, DIFFERENT SHIELDS,
RIGHT RIGHT RIGHT. BUT THOSE LADIES,
THEY BREATHE THE SAME FREQUENCY,
PREFER TATTED LACE, SWIM THE SAME SALT.
YES. THE KINGS WOULD SURELY BEHEAD
THEIR QUEENS IF THE TAWDRY KNOT
WERE UNEARTHED, BUT LIKE AN EYELASH-
WISH, YOU KNOW IT WON'T COME TRUE

AND YOU MAKE IT ANYWAY.
SUDDENLY YOU'RE IN A BED OF LACE
THE COLOR OF SEA SPRAY, MACRAMÉ,
COME AGAIN TOMORROW, SHE SAID.
COVER YOUR FACE.
USE A NEW FAKE NAME.

6. BIRTH OF THE KNIT

On the molten gold wedding ring,
two hands hold each other
like one land before
it's gerrymandered new.

7. BIRTH OF CROCHET

Tear it: the letter you never mailed.
You know the one.
Rip it into pieces,
throw them out the window
of a moving truck.
But the wind laughs
it back in your face,
like a prayer you have no right to say.
Glue it together as you cry,
graft it into your thigh.
It hurts now, but, out of sight,
you will forget to remember.

8. BIRTH OF LACE

I am the loom, the first mechanical arm.
I eat fire. I drink time.
Like flames puppeting shadows,
I am the furnace learning
each inch of the factory floor.
The steps to the basement
are my crooked teeth.
I'm too thirsty to think, too tired to drink,
throat red as regret. Look at my children,
my lace, patterns born in the storm
of gears dancing in time.
My lace, my babies, many-eyed monsters.
What is space but a giant spy?
If you could flatten a cry
what would it look like? Paper?
Thick glue? I am the loom,
you sold my escape path, Sir,
like losing the last match in the box.
It's so hot in here, water hides, color dries.
She's high now, the flame in my womb.
If only fire were a winged creature.
No, Sir, you can't fire me, I've already quit.
I'll spit into your daydream. Don't try me.
What is the purpose of memory
if it can't help you learn what to burn?
Regret is to recollect, repeat the past
like filigree. Look. Queen Anne's Lace
is the color of motif, the hue of what if,
continuous threat of maybe.

As two threads become one you'll find it,
the wish trapped in the lost well; it smells
like a place you haven't been in a decade.
Our story comes together in the sizzled heart
of the mill after a lightning strike. Live wire.
Lace is dry on the tongue but salty
as a sucker punch, appetite of echo.
Lace holds the hesitation of needles,
the swing of every stitch.
No story begins or ends.
Like an itch, it just depends
when it finds you.

DIVE

I can't believe you said we were with the band.
It worked, didn't it?
This place is a dump!
Don't yell. People are looking.
This place is a dive.
No, it's not.
Yes, it is.
Dive is to fall face first.
Um, no. A dive is a shithole. And how to avoid a bullet.
I guess.
If we could stop telling lies for one year, we'd—
We'd what?
Burn Scranton with the lava of truth.
Smartest thing you've said all summer.
Why are you so mean?
I'm just being honest.
This place is a dive. Let's go.
Wild Turkey. Two, actually. Thanks. Here, drink this.
Girls don't drink whiskey! Why did you order that?
Wild Turkey is specific. Specificity makes things more true.
You should've ordered beer.
I got us booze, didn't I?
I guess.
Do you like the whiskey?
It hurts.
That's how you know it's working. Cigarette?
No other girls are smoking.
I lit one for you, so you have to smoke it.
Not really.
Yeah, really. One for me, one for you.

They're both for you.
How's that?
You want to watch me.
Do what?
Hold something between my lips.

5

godspeed says the manager godspeed
is god's speed all that speedy nour wonders
wouldn't god take her time
clouds float so slow they look fast
or is it the other way around
you have nice hands elizabeth says
do i
yes
afternoon flattens shadows
as if nour is being followed
the lace women make
is neither a circle nor a line
like a cave is both inside and outside itself

HINGE

Autumn suspends the world
between leaving and returning.

As a colon glues 11:11,
each hinge is pinned

by the wish of function.
Look at the clues: an old bruise

rooted so deep it eats bone.
You'll hear no gears

on the factory floor,
but colonies of rust

keep looms itchy,
alive. Worn steps

are too pocked
to walk easy

but craters hold rain.
A hole deep enough

can turn one fall day
into mirrors, so many,

if you start counting
you'll never finish.

RUSTY

Anniversary roses
soured the vase water
into a thick moat.
You asked me three times
to toss them: *Sick,*
that smell's sick.
Not dead, not thriving,
but some life they had.
Dusk would not fall.
As thunder punched east
I called for our cat, a rescue
named Rusty because
we thought of nothing better.
But Rusty didn't come.
Wind hammered the walls,
hail hit hard as I yelled
my throat raw.
But she didn't come
when I called her.
She never came again.

FUGUE

True story. The good old days when we were young.
Keats tried to re-weave the rainbow but tied himself in a knot.
> *Open windows, mild breezes, the bright new colorings of Nature*
> *make every woman wish to have her home*
> *as fresh, as clean, as dainty as Springtime itself.*

The Electric City. They just don't make [   ] like they used to.
Keats tried to re-weave the rainbow but only knotted himself.
> *Nothing will freshen up a room so noticeably*
> *and so economically as new curtains.*
> *The wide variety and moderate prices*

True story. The good old days when we were young.
Keats tried to re-weave the rainbow but tied himself in a knot.
> *of Scranton filet nets, lace curtains and Maid-O-Nets*
> *with lace edges have made the frequent changing*
> *of curtains practical and inexpensive.*

The Electric City. They just don't make [   ] like they used to.
Keats tried to re-weave the rainbow but only knotted himself.
> *Follow the styles in curtains*
> *as you do in your own gowns.*
> *THE SCRANTON LACE Co.*

True story. The good old days when we were young.
Keats tried to re-weave the rainbow but tied himself in a knot.
> *THE SCRANTON LACE Co.*
> *Devein the lace from loom. Reset the scream from the throat.*
> *Dismember the memory and let the story go.*

True story. The good old days when we were young.
Keats re-wove the rain's bow. But he knotted himself.
>   *Restretch space within lace like a yawn in the secret lung.*
>   *Return to the beginning, sew the hail back into the cloud.*
>   *Reclaw the cat and hear the murder of wings.*

The Electric City. They just don't make [   ] like they used to.
Keats saved the rainbow, but he could not save us.

THE GREAT LACE HEIST

From the Desk of Sergeant O'Malley, Scranton Precinct #31

Ponder, if you will, how The Lace Factory
could vanish in plain sight. Ten years now
I've lain awake on the eyelid of dusk,
pounded by the clock, wicked tick against tock,
waiting for some insight into The Great Lace Heist.
Per chance it was magic! cried my dear Wife,
or the factory sank! The coal mine inhaled it!
But is not magic a quick trick, succor from gravity?
We possess no such pluck in Scranton—
rot of carbon, stained cavity. No. The pathetic
"illusionist" and his farcical "magic show"
cast a net of smirks. Even miners blind on grog
and hacking black lungs can suss weak stagecraft—
joke of smoke and mirrors, like his zaftig assistant
was actually being sawed in two. Fools. No.
Perhaps angry wind hurled The Lace Factory
into the sea, restless almost as me.
Or a parliament of grand owls snatched it
thinking The Lace a mythic beetle, not knowing
what godly threads danced inside. Oh, mind.
Every possibility, bizarre to mundane,
riddles my brain. Night after night
I sweat myself awake, waiting for some hint,
something I missed, retracing each minute
of that cursed Day, racing to catch up
with what's done and gone.

Memory makes no sense,
one fact contradicts another.
All I know is that the unknown
stays one step ahead.
If I were only fast enough
to keep up with the past.

6
rain breaches
the roof
soaking a scranton lace advert
blurred ink alters the word's meaning
funny how there is no armor against water
elizabeth whispers to nour as they cut lace
nour get a bucket the manager screams nour
get a fucking bucket
but nour is scared of the utility closet
scared of spilling
what is haunted is also preserved
if elizabeth is wet nour cannot tell

A firefly blinks its lightning-eye
once, twice, then disappears.
Every river wind chokes with
ghosts. All fur stays alive even
after the kill. But when we're
gone, we're gone. People who
"have died"—as if death could be
contained in the present perfect
tense—are never coming back.
The Lace Factory as it was is
never coming back, even though
its remains remain. Finitude and
infinity are equally absurd. To
define is to pretend we're finite,
is no middle in end, and

CARPENTER

It was "unfinished," Sean's basement,
seeding the lie that whatever starts
will someday find a tidy ending.

Family pictures hung below
Joseph, Jesus, and John—
portraits in rows neat as funeral seats.

I was 13, the age you're supposed
to want a boy to search your body.
But seven minutes in heaven with him

was seven minutes of phlegm.
I held my breath as he kissed me,
stared at the bridge of his nose.

The closest I've ever been to praying
was fainting, wishing myself out of a room.
In Scranton, queer was neither a cure nor curse.

It didn't exist. Ignore Sean's sister, Sam,
on the floor in her tank-top, painting toenails.
Of all the portraits in their basement

I liked Joseph the best, quiet
carpenter, dull halo instead
of bright gold, every angle a right one,

wood tools so straight. A simple man
with working hands, hiding in plain sight.

LONG AGO AND NOT LONG AT ALL

It was long ago and not long at all when rust began. Rust grows
the way water burns—a ghost with no reason to rush. The real
teases itself into your veins when it rains, and rust waits. Start
the ceremony and rust bends the keys, like the smoke-soaked
walls in the hall of failed incantations. Squeeze out the treble
as red consecrates, penetrates each stare. Rust is the dead need
to stay stable, the hand reaching for railing. Rust is
the = of time + ache, the causality of cyclical pain. Let the
brush-burn hold you, slow and fast, startling as waking
in a rusty, stifling tin. If a second is a word, every hour
is a page in the book never written about the origin of rust
and how long ago and not long at all the air learned to bleed.

PLUMBER

What don't I find in walls?
Shot wiring, toy cars, mummified mice.
I even found a gun wrapped in a towel
tucked in a hole as narrow as a neck.
I slid it out slow, showed Sheriff.
Holy smokes, he said.

The house had been a speakeasy,
linked to the mines by secret tunnels.
Men need whiskey after drilling abyss.
Deep shafts through carbon, one
over another, braided tight as hair.
Police took it down in a raid,
filled each passage with cement.
How men hate being played.

Yeah, cops ruined the fun,
but don't we all have a door
we want kept shut, a dark corridor
we're desperate to seal?

QUICK

In the 1980s, when Saturday was adultspeak for cartoons,
we unrolled ourselves on the living room floor with a plate of
Hot Pockets & glass of Strawberry Quick. Like most sets in
Scranton, our television was housed in a thick wood frame
because watching TV is an art itself. We poured ourselves into
the Looney Tunes like painters etching self-portraits. From
the second we woke until Dad yelled *dinner!* we lay side by
side, glued to the floor, so close to the TV we fogged the glass.
The musty rug's gold swans stretched & sighed underneath us
like our winged shadows—doppelgängers of doppelgängers.
We reenacted the high jinks of Tweety & Bugs & the Dancing
Frog before the scenes were over, keeping the joke alive, our
tiny identical voices trying to mirror the vocal ticks that made
Bugs Bugs & Me me & Her her. Who were we entertaining back
then? Ourselves or each other? During the commercials we
raced to the kitchen, nuked more Hot Pockets, & returned to
our glowing swans careful not to spill our shared glass of pink
Quick that we refilled together—one twin holding the glass,
the other twin stirring. We sprinted as the Roadrunner zooms,
even now, from Wiley Coyote against the arid red I thought
was trapped in animated cells until it appeared in Mom's
glossy art book, a famous painting of a wilting clock.
But Dali was wrong. Time can't melt or spill down a cliff.
Time roars only forward.

AFTER THE FIRE

Bruises map where heat
Pushed too hard.
Charred wires,
Melted rugs.
An unbroken line
Where fire
Crawled the wall—
Up, up, up—to the duct.
Smoke snuck everywhere,
Choked the peach tree.
The cedar you carved
In the yard
With your first love,
Now a pond of needles,
Like the shadow of a girl
Hiding under a sink
During the alarm.
As smoke clears,
You kneel in rubble,
Searching for your
Camera. You find it
Under bricks, layer
Leaking layer. Your
Lens is intact but cracked
In the middle.
When you hold it close
It shows you everything.
When you hold it close
It cuts you.

IN OLD HAVANA I FELT NEW

In Old Havana I felt new. Isn't that a saying?
          Except you cannot feel new
when you're cut in half. In Cuba, everything began for me.
          Or it ended.

We sailed from Nassau in a steamship: teenage me
          and a girl with blue-grey eyes.
I think I'm gay I whispered at the sticky marble bar where
          Reinaldo Arenas

may or may not have opened his body for the first time.
          I wanted to be myself
for the first time. Clouds veined with storm. The blue-grey girl
          and I practiced Spanish

by scribbling on bar napkins. Sólo amigos, she wrote. Just friends.
          I didn't know how
to gender words, make verbs agree. I crave the day rain on a mirror
          spells nothing at all.

If we can't see through eyelids, why could I swear she watched
          me as I slept?
If we can't see through eyelids, why could I sense her leaning
          as I pretended to sleep?

In Old Havana I cried so hard I couldn't see. She knew how
          to hail a taxi. In the back
of a pink Chevrolet, windows low, Malecón's salt wind.
          You need to stop falling

for straight girls, she said. *We'll stay friends, though, okay?*
        Of course we didn't.
I'm not hot-tempered, I'm cold-blooded. I can almost
        stand in the deep end.

Like a honeycomb, the more you turn a memory
        the more doors you find.
In the gold field we ran from bees. We need light
        to see color, but light itself is color.

Even now as I let cold mint burn my tongue I think
        of Old Havana.
Even now I could tell you the girl's eyes were the blue-grey
        of a ghost wave,

how her blond hair fell against her jaw, how her
        bottom lip was as soft
as old lace. Not because I held her face, but because
        I wanted to.

THE LENGTHS

if

you

want

them

to

join

you

you

must

be

willing

to

go

alone

7
folding lace
nour looks into elizabeth's eyes
when she says
trust the blade
trust how it cuts
but also trust that you can jump
betrayal of gravity
or something like that

CONSIDER THE FLOWER

This flower stains my fingers.
That flower blooms at night.
When I sleep near this flower my dreams are laced
the way minerals in ice change the taste of whiskey.
Instead of words, send that flower for mercy.
I planted this flower after you left,
but too big it bloomed, too fast,
its heart broke its shell, toppled itself.
How is it fair?
The stem near sun climbs
while the one in shadow
is surprised by its weight,
can't get itself right,
like a torn sail in a sudden storm.

GAS STATION BATHROOM OFF RT. 6

You can't identify the color of toilet water making Kate gag.

You can't pretend you don't notice the whisper of cocaine
dusting Kate's left nostril.

You can't not smile as Kate tries to read a map sideways.

You can't agree with the notion of north or south when
the planet never stops spinning long enough to measure.

You can't count the hours you or your wallet have been
awake, George Washington's eyes eternally wide open.

the eye until it finds its hand holding the thread chases the

WHAT IF FALLING WASN'T FALLING?

What if falling wasn't falling?
Everything lifts
as I stay in place,
perfectly still.
I think of this as I leave
work, gulls scream
out of sight,
high as blood-pressure
on a turbulent flight.
Like the trick of direction
in a painting of rain
or a rowboat floating
on sunset's flaming,
as I look closely
everything reverses.
Why do possibilities scare me?
Am I so numb, so un-young
I keep myself distracted?
I can't recall
the last time I made time
for a clockless walk,
phoneless wonder.
Maybe I'm not sinking;
it's the waves
that are jumping,
the globe spinning.
Look. I can open
one eye at a time.
No. Each eye
opens me.

AT THE B&B

         even the sink is haunted.
The faucet, a reaper's scythe,
tiny door bricked up behind.
3AM, too thirsty to sleep,
startled by my reflection.
I pour water into the cup of my hands.
One hundred years ago, did a woman
avoid this same mirror, hold cold
water in her palms like a small,
hollow organ? Did she, too,
worry about worry lines,
hate how her left eyelid
slid heavier than her right?
Did she wonder about the woman
one hundred years before?
All of us at the gray mirror,
washing away each year
until we're facing each other.

NIAGARA

She is not like you or me. She's not an early-to-bed,
        early-to-rise.

She is a wolf in heat, so don't get cute. Don't try anything.
        She sleeps light.

She is the cousin of rain who is the aunt of thunder and
        mother of a knife.

She is the end and beginning of the forest.
        Watch her swallow red birds mid-flight.

She is usually the late one, the latest, the last one at the bar,
        every single time.

She is not one who can be dressed-down by a summer storm
        or blue moonrise.

She is the Devil's Throat, the Angel's Eye, ultraviolet itching
        your ears.

She is the woman you want but can't touch, restless,
        elegant as tears.

8

nour rubs fresh lace against her cheek
the softness stuns her
try not to want or not want says father ted
that way you won't be disappointed
tension cables in the loom room
fan out like the vertebrae of wind
gathering strength with each gale
if nour could only lean out of the factory window and fall
she would feel this

WE ARE GREATER

we are greater than the sum of our parts
but how can i be greater than all the parts
inside me when i don't know
where i begin or end
perhaps i am greater than the cogito
ergo sum or maybe what makes you great
is how you play the game
& how you breathe through pain
but what if the pain is breathing you
& you are the sum's marionette
which is why i summarily suggest that
sure the sun sits in the center
of the celestial sea & planets revolve
around the same sun but how many
secret suns are spinning around
those planets which themselves swim
so fast they are unseen like the um
between words because the hum
is louder than the total of every word
i see life through this lens
because i am a gemini
part summer mostly winter
& not just any winter
surprise winter like the donner party
when winter tricked them because it could
no the donner party wasn't much of a partyparty
like a dance party or pizza party
bones & ears were served at the donner party
but just as every season leaks into the next
that winter bled into summer

wind writing its own geometry
but more importantly we are here
in whatever circle whatever equation
this is & though i would never imply
that wings are greater than the plane
a factory cannot grind
without its smallest gears
i know i am nothing special
but i want to be great
or at least good
because science says
that since we are married
you are a part of me
& i am a part of you

9

where is lebanon elizabeth asks
across many oceans nour says
it sounds like something at the factory
what do you mean
ribbon lebanon ribbon lebanon
i guess
you're a long way from home
but scranton is my home
not with that name
i guess
nour looks at the cog's impossibly tiny teeth
how could something so small
control every rhythm

THE TALKING SPECIES

the folly of it
words pouring
pouring
from our mouths

what trees must think

FORGIVENESS

What is forgiveness, a rite or response?
If, as Bachelard says, ideas are invented

as correctives to the past, all art asks
forgiveness for one sin or another.

Sorry. Sorry.
I'm so sorry.

I don't think I can do this any more.
All my life chasing someone else's wish

of a wish, like being homesick
for a bedroom in a black-and-white movie.

YOU WILL HEAR A WOBBLE IN THE VOICE

You will hear a swerve in the voice as she explains
why she never had a baby. Finally happy in her skin,
she testifies. No itchy clocks. No void to fill.
Still. You'll hear her voice tear as she clarifies
it's not because she's gay. Today, lesbian moms
are as de rigueur as gourmet salt and Pilates.
You will hear a wobble in the voice, though her eyes
belie it, as she itemizes the winsome men who,
year after year, offered themselves as donors and dads.
Like a striped warbler you cannot see even when
she is quite near, there's a clear stumble in her voice
when she tells you she does not regret her choice.
But the word *regret* fumbles, like a hiccup, trips
on its laces, means I'm sorry, I fucked up, remorse.

CRACK

The guest room door is cracked and it's not that bad except
in the winter when the wood contracts because cold air is
pressure. In the winter the wood contracts from the crow-
bar of pressure and we can see inside the guest room to
the far wall where a crib would fit. If we chose that path a
crib could fit, you say, but no pressure. In the middle of the
guest room door is a crack and it's not all bad except when
it's cold the wood contracts and the crack gets worse and
we can see through to the far wall. No pressure, you say,
but we can redo the guest room into a nursery. What do
you think? I don't know. What do you think? It is the
coldest room of the house. Instead of the space inside the
room I stare at the edge of the crack and say this door
is not broken but it's not perfect either. What do you think?
I don't know.

10
october is a beautiful month
october is a beautiful mouth
so what do you do on weekends elizabeth asks
i don't have time for leisure
too bad the church fair is on saturday
oh
well anyway you have a nice hand
a nice what
with the needle elizabeth says you hold it in the right way

THE PLACE YOU LOVE AND LEAVE

Any place you love and leave
takes a piece of you,
hides it under its moss.
You'll never not miss it,
reaching in the dark,
like tongueing
the raw grave
of a pulled molar.
But that piece—the you
still there—grew and
grew into a yew tree.
You hate it, this ache
that never ceases.
Is there any inch of us left
that hasn't been cut open
by lust at least once?
Longing is the only chord
that begs to be played
from the inside out,
but no fingers can reach.
No, you'll never go back.
But now the hawk
has a branch,
a nest of her own,
a reason to go home.

FIRST DOOR

The day your mom lost
her balance, you flew
to Oklahoma. I stayed home
and slept with windows open.
On the phone I used the word
miracle to describe the woods—
walking alone—fractals of fern,
rippling moss. Every hole is a door
in the forest floor. No wonder
it's where fairy tales were born.
Each leaf an eye. Every branch a beak.
When you told me how you carried
your mother room to room
because she could not stand,
I thought *miracle*, not because
of sleeplessness or atrophied limbs,
but now your mom, your first door,
is walking through you.
It will never be okay again,
but the lie feels good
so I let myself believe it,
the way I imagine jumping
into that fresco, grabbing
Adam and God's wrists,
making their fingertips touch.
It's real, right, a miracle?
Why else would the word exist?
A word that we need
to hear ourselves say,
a word that has to
leave our lips
to make us smile.

11
nour and elizabeth stand closer
closer
their output has increased
more tablecloths more drapes more lace
have you ever held a frog elizabeth asks
no i don't get outside much
i held a frog once its legs
were so strong it pried my fingers open
oh
i'd like to be pried open nour thinks
or prayed open

THE LOST ART OF GETTING LOST

Once upon a time there was time.
Once upon a time there was Off.
Now hands roll over screens
like spells cast too fast to notice the gaze,
glaze hardening into lacquer.
Warbler: I've been waiting.
Now you claim the tree stump,
sound as a compass.
Chin-down, scrolling, I search
to confirm you're you
and when I look up, you're gone,
white throat dissolved in clouds
like a memory of skywriting.
Buy the Bird Finder App. Subscribe to Nature Now.
GPS routes the straightest path,
though a wrong turn would lead into a shy forest
blinking with purple berries, violets, mayflower.
A set of high wings pour a shadow so thick
it drinks moss. I never knew ink could fly.
Where did it go, the desire
to not know, keep knots tied?
Afraid of getting lost we're losing ourselves.
If Google's grip slipped and
maps quit Northing and Southing
we'd hover and flip like lunar walkers.
Which makes me wonder:
what would that freckle on your neck
look like upside down?

RUBE GOLDBERG

The fastest path between A and B? Screw it.
You haven't seen C since last May and D,
well, D is wild after a Pinot Noir or two.
Don't sprint. Take the circuitous way,
rickety ride on the Wonder Wheel;
from the sky, see how the city
dilates like a mood-swing.
A zillion electrons collide
in one millimeter of glitter;
it shines like pain in your eyes.
Who can rig up a gizmo to say
the hard words, cobble a clock that lies?
Give me the fucking superglue. I'll try.
Yep, technology's sexy and wafer-thin,
but it's the snowstorm—when we sit
together and watch it—that makes
the best heat, throws the most light.

BLESSING IN DISGUISE

Is it rude to think about sex
In the dentist's chair!
Lately I wonder if
Right or wrong even exist!
It was Heidegger who said
All perception is situational!
Or was it the frog, Kermit!
In Scranton we were desperate
For a 50¢ moustache
From the vending machine
So I could order whiskey in disguise!
We combed the sticky floor for coins!
We didn't find any but you looked so
Fearless and regal casing the bar
Like a ruby thief in a silent movie!
Let's break into the dentist's tonight!
The Nitrous Oxide might kill us
But how sweet it would be
To die on top of you
Laughing!

12

desire is like the sun elizabeth says
always there
even when it's not
do you hear that
i don't hear anything nour says
don't you hear the fire
no i have to go home and pray
in the labyrinth of the ear
all realities co-exist
with my face near hers nour thinks
it is the same scarred moon
the sacred never changes
it's we who change
just us
just
us

VALENTINE'S DAY

Enough with red hearts already. Look at the dark arc
around the heart, the way it inhales like undertow.

The heart has no pleasing shape. Not like the key you've lost.
Lick inside a lock to taste what it's really like to be needed.

Today, all the women I've ever tricked, kicked in the face,
snake the streets in a parade, shiny as an axe rewriting wood.

Squint and the gold highway turns to code, prison-break
of braided sheets. The quiet before the alarm is my ringtone.

See? See how pathetic! How quick I short-circuit,
plug into the wrong socket. So fast it all fries.

How do we plan for all the blown fuses life promises?
Flip every switch now? Wait for the blackout? Buy candles?

Today, you hold my charred heart in your long fingers,
dust off the ash. Maybe that's what makes this—us—

different. You love me in a broken world.
You stay, not despite my sadness, but because of it.

CORK

Don't shoot! you screamed. New Year's Eve on the porch,
too hammered to stand, snowflakes glowed in my fake
eyelashes like the halo of concussion. I pointed
the champagne bottle at the yard, scared as a dare accepted.
The cork shot high then disappeared in snow.
We swore we'd never settle as midnight ticked us
one year older. Most of my life I wanted to be the cork,
explode hard, held by nothing, not even night—
moon-white—something clean to tear through.
As snow melted in March, I found the cork, intact
on cold grass, surprising as if a fish crawled ashore.
Why am I shocked when things work out?
You and me, a champagne cork the shape
of the rusty keyhole we never tried opening.
Maybe I lost it. Maybe I never had the key.
I could pick the lock, but only if you help me.

13
nour faces the loom
or does the loom faces her
she isn't sure
she is sure that she stole elizabeth's lace
slid her fingers in the spool
pulled a thread
it's ruined elizabeth cries
it's ruined
elizabeth is fired
but please i must work please no please
the manager walks elizabeth out
it's ruined
everything is ruined
but now nour has one piece
of elizabeth
something real
something to hold close
to her mouth
inside the seam
of night

ACKNOWLEDGMENTS

Grateful acknowledgment to the following publications where these poems originally appeared (some in altered forms):

Belmond Magazine (2015): "Niagra"

The Bloodstone Review (2015): "Helicopter"

The Common (Amherst College, 2015): "The Lost Art of Getting Lost"

The Four Quarters Magazine (2015): "We are Greater" and "The Place You Love and Leave"

Girls Like You (Clemson University Press, 2015): "Avon"

Sounding East (Salem State University, 2015): "Rube Goldberg"

The South Carolina Review (Clemson University Press, 2016): "Dive" and "Gutted"

The Tishman Review (2016): "Plumber" and "Scranton Lace"

Tupelo Press's 30/30 Project (2015): "Consider the Flower," "Hinge," "The Lengths," and "What if Falling Wasn't Falling?"

The Wisconsin Review (2016): "Runaway"

The first three italicized stanzas in "Fugue" are taken from an original Scranton Lace Company curtain advertisement.

Two lyrics in *Cutters* are from the Dire Straits song "Money for Nothing."

A lyric in "Blue Monday" is from the New Order song "Blue Monday."

Notes

THE SCRANTON LACE COMPANY

Pennsylvania's Scranton Lace Company was a producer of
fine textiles for nearly 120 years. The company's facility has
been empty since it was shuttered in 2002. Plans are uncertain
for the factory that was, during its halcyon, a source of
pride in my hometown of Scranton. Though it is a real place
intertwined with personal histories—indeed, I, my family,
friends, neighbors, and thousands of other people have deep
connections to Scranton Lace—these poems merge the lived
and imagined to investigate the architecture of a derelict space.
The structures of internalized homophobia that I built in my
youth, while they no longer serve me, are still hazardous and
strangely comforting, like the manufacturing plant that is no
longer in use. How do we dismantle forms that now fail to
fulfill their original functions? Is there utility in the obsolete?
Stitched in each poem is the crosstalk of synesthesia and the
push-pull tension inherent in personal and urban reinvention.

—Margot Douaihy

A COLLABORATIVE ILLUSTRATION PROCESS

All of the illustrations in *Scranton Lace* incorporate prints made
with lace manufactured at the Scranton Lace Factory during
its operation. The nature of the printing process highlights the
extraordinary intricacies of the patterns while also adding a layer
of deterioration. The book's cover shows the facade of the factory
and original signage that reflect the damage within; exterior and
interior mirror each other. The overprint of lace dissolves the
factory in finery. We wanted to explore the concept of graceful
decomposition, a place elegantly being effaced by itself.

In "Stage Directions," we were interested in subverting the conventional notion of stage directions as literal guidelines, and instead using them to suggest a liminal, queer, and female space. There is a narrative arc sewn into the book, a story of love and loss. The two characters are imaginary female factory workers—a Lebanese immigrant, Nour, and coworker, Elizabeth. They interact with the lace, they are created from it (their dresses are ink and lace), and they are undone by it.

The disappearing poem (page 50) is verse written with illegibility as a goal. It appears either to dissolve into lace or be absorbed by it, allowing the riddle of textile to assert itself.

In "the thread chases the eye" (page 64), a rosette of Scranton Lace stitches a lyric together in a perfect loop. There is no beginning, ending, or middle, challenging the insistence on linear narrative. We believe this echoes the nonlinear life of nostalgia.

In all of these collaborations, we used the product—which was skillfully made by real people and has been sitting in a box, unused—to honor it and tell a new story about a once grand, now abandoned edifice. We held the lace, wore it, hung it, looked through it, tore it, and dipped it in acrylic ink to make relief prints. By utilizing the textile as both the instrument and the canvas, Scranton Lace becomes process and product.

—Margot Douaihy and Bri Hermanson

CPSIA information can be obtained
at www.ICGtesting.com
Printed in the USA
BVHW02s0342100418
512845BV00013B/208/P